LETTS POCKET GUIDE TO

SEASHELLS

The most common species of European
seashells described and illustrated in
colour

Eleanor Lawrence and Sue Harniess

Front cover illustration: Queen Scallop

This edition first published 1991
by Charles Letts & Co Ltd
Diary House, Borough Road,
London SE1 1DW

'Letts' is a registered trademark of
Charles Letts (Scotland) Ltd

This edition produced under licence by
Malcolm Saunders Publishing Ltd, London
Editorial concept by Pamela Forey

© 1991 this edition Atlantis Publications Ltd

All rights reserved. No part of this publication
may be reproduced, stored in a retrieval system,
or transmitted, in any form or by any means,
electronic, mechanical, photocopying, recording
or otherwise without the prior written permission of
the copyright holder.

British Library Cataloguing in Publication Data
Lawrence, Eleanor
    Seashells.
    1. Marine molluscs. Shells
    I. Title II. Harniess, Sue
    594.0471

    ISBN 1 85238 114 0

Contents

Introduction

Few people come home from the seaside without picking up a few seashells. With this book you can now put a name to them.

Seashells belong to a group of animals called molluscs — to which land snails and slugs also belong. In this book we have also added a few barnacles, which are not molluscs but crustaceans, relatives of crabs and lobsters.

Most of the shells in this book live on the shores between low and high tides or in shallow coastal waters. European seashells are generally not as large or brightly coloured as their tropical relatives, but many are very decorative, and a number are good to eat.

The shell protects the animal from predators and, for those that live on the shore, from the pounding of the surf and from drying out when exposed. When the animals die their shells remain for long afterwards, and are washed up on the beach.

Beaches are the easiest place to look for shells to collect, as both shore-living and offshore shells will be washed up. You can also look for the living animals, especially at low tide. But watch the tides, especially on rocky coasts where it is easy to get cut off.

How to use this book

The book is divided into six sections, based on the form of the shell. The sections are **Gastropod Shells**, **Bivalve Shells**, **Nautiloids**, **Chitons**, **Tusk Shells** and **Barnacles**. Each section is indicated by a different coloured band at the top of the page. To identify your shell, first decide which section it belongs to, using the information in the *Guide to Identification* which follows. It is possible that you will not be able to find the exact shell in this book, although most of the common European shells are illustrated. But you will certainly be able to find a very similar one of the same family.

Guide to identification

First decide to which section your shell belongs.

Gastropods These animals have a single, large shell which may be spirally coiled, dome-shaped, cap-shaped or cone-shaped. Spirally coiled shells are usually twisted into a helix but some are coiled in a flat plane, and in others the helix opens out into an irregularly twisted form. The last whorl of the coil, the body whorl, is the largest, the one in which the animal lives. The shells may be simple and unadorned or may have complex decorations of spines, knobs and sculpturing.

Bivalves These animals have a shell consisting of two more-or-less equal halves (valves), joined by a hinge. In life, the two valves are closed by powerful muscles, but after the animal has died the two valves often become separated or spread out.

Nautiloids These are relatives of the octopus and squid. Only one species lives in European waters. The shells are superficially like those of a gastropod.

Chitons Easily recognized by the eight, often overlapping, plates which make up the shell. They form a wide band along the back of the animal and are held in place by an encircling fleshy girdle. Chitons are usually found alive.

Tusk Shells These animals have hollow tubular, tusk-shaped shells which are open at both ends. The shell tapers from the bottom to the top; in life the head of the animal emerges from the larger, bottom opening. Since they live in deep water, these animals are not usually seen alive but their empty shells are washed up onto beaches.

Barnacles These are not molluscs but crustaceans. Their 'shell' is composed of a number of plates. Most barnacles encrust rocks, the bottom of boats, other shells, etc.

Making a positive identification

Within the first two sections shells are sequenced by size from the smallest to the largest, to enable you to find your particular shell easily. The size of each shell is given at the top of the page, together with a size symbol for easy reference (see Fig. 1). For most gastropods, the size refers to the height from the tip of the spire to the bottom of the shell; however in some shells, like ormers and limpets, it is the length of the shell which has been measured, and in some flattened shells the width has been given. This has been indicated wherever relevant. For bivalves, chitons and tusk shells, the size refers to the length of the shell from the front to hind end.

Characteristic features

The first two boxes are designed to be used together to enable you to make a quick identification. The first box gives details which identify the shell as a particular species, as a *European Cowrie* for example, rather than any other kind of cowrie. The second box provides additional information of a more general nature, which may be true of other

Key to size symbols

	Gastropods		Bivalves
▪	up to 2cm/¾in	●	up to 3cm/1in
●	up to 5cm/2in	●	up to 5cm/2in
●	up to 10cm/4in	●	up to 10cm/4in
●	up to 15cm/6in	●	up to 20cm/8in
●	up to 30cm/12in	●	up to 30cm/12in

cowries as well. Where relevant, the second box also contains information about the economic significance of the shell, whether you can eat it, etc.

Habitat and distribution
The habitat in which a shell is found, and its distribution in European waters are important clues to its identity. There are four basic areas of distribution in Europe: Mediterranean, Atlantic, Channel and North Sea. The distribution of each shell is given in a map in the illustration and more detailed information on habitat and occurrence is given in the box. The main habitat division is between those shells that live on or among rocks and those that live in sand. This box also includes information about the behaviour of the living shell.
T = throughout the area

Similar and related species
In the fourth box are given some shells that might be confused with the featured species. Those printed in **bold** type are illustrated, either as featured species or in the *Other Common Species* sections; those printed in ordinary type are not.

Other common species
At the end of the gastropod and bivalve sections you will find pages of other common species. These are generally less common or less obvious than the featured seashells.

Now you are ready to use this book. It is designed to fit in your pocket, so take it with you on your next trip to the coast and don't forget to check your findings on the checklist provided. Looking for animals is an exciting pastime, but please remember that these are living animals and leave them on the beach where they live. Hundreds of creatures live on the shore, many of them under rocks and stones, where they are protected from waves and drying out; if you turn over stones to look at what is underneath, please make sure you turn them back again so that the animals are not killed by sea or sun. Look for the empty shells cast up by the waves and take them home. Photograph the others.

Fig. 2 Specimen page

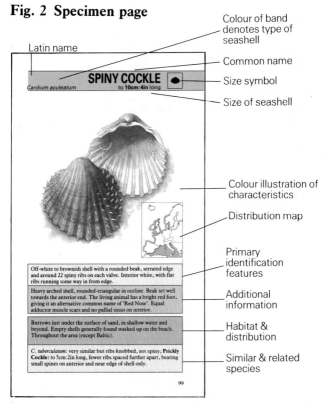

Colour of band denotes type of seashell

Latin name

Common name

SPINY COCKLE

Cardium aculeatum   to 10cm:4in long

Size symbol

Size of seashell

Colour illustration of characteristics

Distribution map

Primary identification features

Off-white to brownish shell with a rounded beak, serrated edge and around 22 spiny ribs on each valve. Interior white, with flat ribs running some way in from edge.

Additional information

Heavy arched shell, rounded-triangular in outline. Beak set well towards the anterior end. The living animal has a bright red foot, giving it an alternative common name of 'Red Nose'. Equal adductor muscle scars and no pallial sinus on interior.

Habitat & distribution

Burrows just under the surface of sand, in shallow water and beyond. Empty shells generally found washed up on the beach. Throughout the area (except Baltic).

Similar & related species

C. tuberculatum: very similar but ribs knobbed, not spiny; **Prickly Cockle**: to 5cm:2in long, fewer ribs spaced further apart, bearing small spines on anterior and near edge of shell only.

99

Glossary of terms

Aperture The opening of a shell in a gastropod.

Apex The tip of the spire in a gastropod.

Beak The apex of the valve in a bivalve shell. Often curved towards the front end.

Byssus A cluster of hair-like threads found in some bivalves which anchor the animal to the substrate. Such animals have a byssal notch, a hole in the shell through which the byssus passes.

Columella The thick central axis of a gastropod shell. It often extends beyond the aperture and forms the siphonal canal. In many shells there are folds or ridges on the columella where it borders the aperture.

Growth lines Lines in the shells of bivalves and gastropods that mark former stages of growth in the shell.

Ligament A brown horny structure which, together with the hinge, links the two valves together in bivalves. It is usually found outside the hinge.

Longitudinal ribs Ridges which run from the apex of the shell to the aperture in a gastropod.

Mantle The fleshy covering of the living animal which lines and manufactures the shell. In most molluscs it remains inside the shell but in some gastropods, like the cowries, it extends out and over the shell.

Muscle scars The round scars on the inside of a bivalve shell marking the position of attachment of the muscles which open and close the shell.

Operculum A horny or calcareous plate which closes the aperture in many gastropods. It is attached to the foot of the animal.

Pallial sinus A tongue-shaped indentation of the line connecting front and rear muscle scars on the inside of some bivalve shells. A useful identification feature, the pallial sinus is always to the rear end of the shell.

Periostracum A shiny, hairy or velvety covering to the shell which is found on many gastropods and bivalves. It may be thin or thick and is often a different colour to the shell itself. The periostracum is often worn away in places, especially on dead shells.

Shoulder Flattened area found at the top of some whorls in some gastropods.

Siphonal canal or **groove** A channel at the base of the aperture in some gastropds, through which the siphon protrudes in the living animal. The siphon is an extension of the mantle which carries water in and out of the shell.

Spire The whorls above the body whorl in a gastropod.

Suture The line between one whorl and the next.

Umbilicus A hole found at the base of the columella in some gastropods.

Valve One of the two halves of a shell in bivalves. The valves are connected together along the upper margin by a hinge (usually toothed) and a ligament.

Varix (pl. **varices**) A large longitudinal ridge in some gastropods, for example tritons, which represents the former position of the lip of the aperture.

Whorl One turn of the shell in a gastropod. The body whorl is the lowermost and largest.

Gastropod

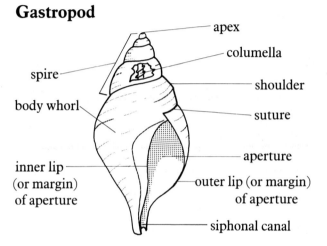

- apex
- columella
- spire
- shoulder
- body whorl
- suture
- aperture
- inner lip (or margin) of aperture
- outer lip (or margin) of aperture
- siphonal canal

Bivalve

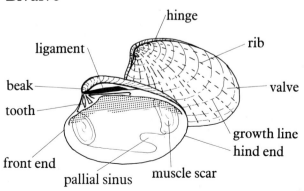

- hinge
- ligament
- rib
- beak
- valve
- tooth
- growth line
- hind end
- front end
- pallial sinus
- muscle scar

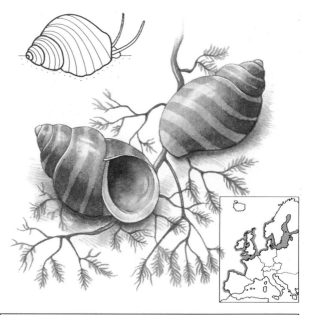

Fragile semitransparent greenish-yellow shell, usually with red-brown banding. A small deep umbilical groove (the 'chink') runs alongside the shelf-like inner lip of aperture.

A thin smooth shell with around 5 well-marked whorls. Rather conical in shape with a pointed spire. Aperture oval with no siphonal groove.

Lower shore and in shallow water below low tide level, on feathery red seaweeds. Atlantic, Channel, North Sea and western Baltic.

Periwinkles; Necklace Shells.

ROUGH PERIWINKLE

Littorina saxatilis to **8mm:⁵⁄₁₆in** high

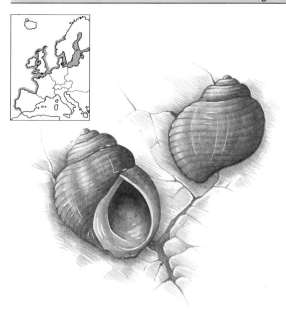

Variably coloured shell, reddish-brown to black, rough to the touch, with 6–9 well-marked rounded whorls and a pointed apex. Outer lip of aperture meets the body at right angles.

Thick shell with a ridged and grooved surface. Aperture round with no siphonal groove. No umbilicus. This periwinkle can breathe air.

Lives in crevices and on stones on upper and upper middle rocky shores, feeding on seaweeds. Atlantic, Channel, North Sea and western Baltic.

Edible Periwinkle; Small Periwinkle; Dog Whelk: aperture has a siphonal grove.

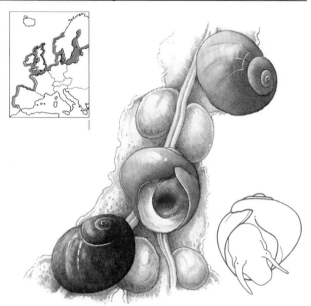

Smooth rounded shell with a flattened spire, the last whorl making up most of the height. Colour ranges from orange to yellow, green, red, brown or black, sometimes banded.

A small solid shell with a large round aperture turned out at the edge and no umbilicus or siphonal groove. On closer inspection the apparently smooth surface is finely sculptured.

Lives in the intertidal zone on sheltered rocky shores, amongst brown seaweeds, on which it feeds, and in rock pools. Atlantic, Channel, North Sea and Baltic.

Other **periwinkles** have pointed spires; **Banded Chink Shell, Necklace Shells:** have an umbilicus; **Dog Whelk** and other **whelks:** have a siphonal groove.

Gibbula cineraria — to **1·25cm : ½in** high

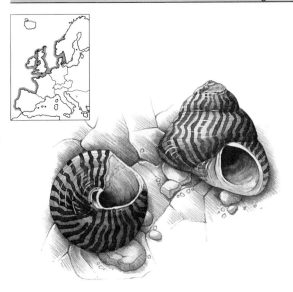

Greyish conical shell marked with closely spaced thin diagonal darker grey stripes. The apex is often worn showing silver underneath. Small umbilicus.

Solid flat-bottomed shell of up to 7 whorls with a pointed spire. Interior of aperture white. In the live animal the aperture is closed by a spirally marked lid (operculum).

Very common on middle and lower rocky shores, on rocks, under stones and on seaweeds, on which it feeds. Atlantic, Channel, North Sea.

Purple Top Shell; Thick Top Shell; Grooved Top Shell;
Gibbula magus; G. divaricata; Monodonta turbinata.

PURPLE TOP SHELL

to **1·25cm: ½in** high

Gibbula umbilicalis

Conical shell of up to 7 whorls with a somewhat flattened apex and bulging sides. Greenish-grey background marked with broad purple diagonal stripes. Large umbilicus.

Solid flat-bottomed shell rather flattened in appearance. The apex when worn shows silvery mother-of-pearl. In the live animal the aperture is blocked by a spirally marked lid (operculum).

Lives on rocks on the middle shore, locally common on the Atlantic and Channel coasts.

Grey Top Shell; Thick Top Shell; Grooved Top Shell;
Gibbula magus; G. divaricata; Monodonta turbinata.

EUROPEAN COWRIE

Trivia monacha   to **1·5cm**:⅝**in** long

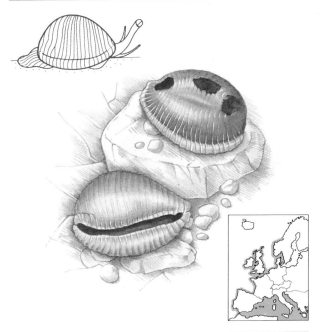

Pretty white or pink shell with 20–25 delicate transverse ridges and 3 purple-brown spots on the back.

A small solid shell, with a slit-like aperture underneath. Ridges extend over lips of aperture. Surface usually shiny, but shells washed up on the beach may be whitened and dulled. In the live animal a fleshy mantle covers most of the shell.

On rocky shores, at and below low water mark, on rocks and beneath stones, feeding on sea squirts and other ascidians. Throughout the area.

The Northern Cowrie (*T. arctica*) is generally smaller and has no spots. Atlantic, Channel and North Sea; **False Simnia:** Mediterranean; other **cowries; Margin Shell.**

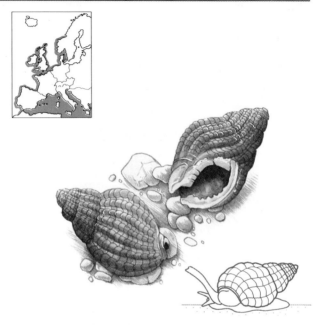

Brownish shell with 8–10 rounded whorls. Strongly marked longitudinal ribs are crossed by thinner ridges. Oval aperture has a thick outer lip and a short siphonal groove.

Small solid shell, elongated conical in shape. Brownish in colour with darker brown bands and a brown blotch at base. Individual rounded egg capsules similar to those of Dog Whelk may also be found attached to rocks.

A scavenger, common in rocky or stony areas, on the lower shore or in shallow water below low tide level. Mediterranean, Atlantic, Channel and North Sea.

Netted Dog Whelk; Sting Winkle; other **whelks.** The siphonal groove distinguishes it from many other small similarly shaped shells.

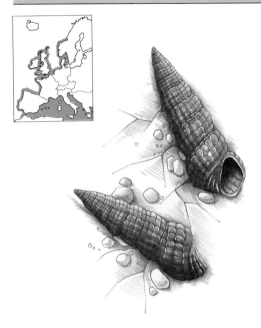

Narrow pointed reddish-brown shell of up to 16 whorls, each ornamented with 4 rows of beading.

Small solid shell with a round aperture, slightly notched at base, and with no umbilicus. Often found washed up in large quantities along tide line.

Common on the lower shore and in shallow water under stones and rocks. Throughout the area.

A careful examination of the drifts of tiny shells washed up on some beaches will discover several other small (sometimes very small) needle-shaped shells which are difficult to distinguish from each other.

BLUE-RAYED LIMPET
to **1·5cm**:⅝**in** long   *Patina pellucida*

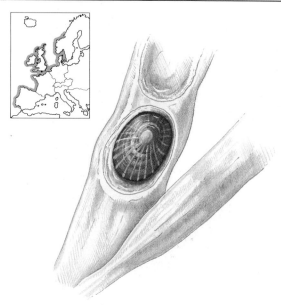

Smooth brown translucent shell, boat-shaped, with lines of bright blue dashes radiating from apex. Older specimens are duller in colour.

A delicate shell becoming more solid with age. Some individuals have rough shells with numerous paler blue rays and have been considered as a separate variety (*laevis*). Interior of shell smooth and brownish.

Common on lower rocky shores, often found on oarweeds (laminaria) on which it feeds making typical hollows on the stalks. Atlantic, Channel and North Sea.

None, the blue rays are distinctive.

SLIT LIMPET ·

Emarginula reticulata

to **1·5cm:⅝in** long

Greyish-white ribbed shell with distinctive slit in front edge and apex slightly curved over. In the living animal a tubular siphon protrudes through the slit.

Shallow conical oval shell, with longitudinal ribs radiating from apex and connected by short horizontal ribbing. Apex situated towards the back end. Colour varies from greyish to greenish or yellow.

Quite common on rocks on the lower shore and beyond to a depth of 60m:200ft. Throughout the area.

Do not mistake these limpet shells for one half of a bivalve shell. A smaller species (*E. elongata*) with a more curved apex is also found in the Mediterranean; **Keyhole Limpets.**

23

VELVET SHELL
to **2cm**:**¾in** long

Velutina velutina

Brownish pink mottled shell with only 3 whorls of which the body whorl is by far the largest, opening in a large round aperture.

Thin fragile smooth oval shell. In life it is covered with a pale brown velvety layer and is also obscured almost completely by the thick yellow mantle.

An uncommon shell, found in sheltered places on rocks and stones on the lower shore and to a depth of 50m:165ft, feeding on soft coral (*Alcyonium*). Atlantic, Channel and North Sea.

Violet Sea Snails; Necklace Shells.

Pinkish- or brownish-grey barrel-shaped shell of 7 whorls with yellow or white bands. Smooth except for fine grooves at base. Twisted columella on inner lip of aperture.

Thin shell with a large body whorl and short pointed spire, and an elongated aperture narrowing sharply at one end. In life it is almost entirely enclosed by the animal (a sea-slug) which can, however, completely withdraw into it.

In sandy bays, burrowing in sand or mud on the lower shore and in shallow water. Mediterranean, Atlantic, Channel and North Sea.

Mediterranean Cone Shell; Mitre-shell; Dove Shell; small **whelks** and **periwinkles.**

MITRE-SHELL
to **2cm**:¾**in** high

Mitra ebenus

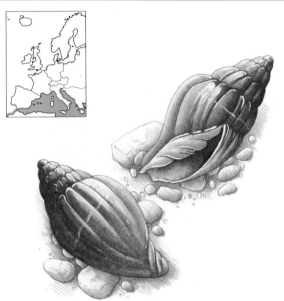

Glossy dark brown or blackish shell of around 9 well-defined whorls, with a pointed spire and a spiral yellow line. Fine sculpturing on surface.

Solid spindle-shaped shell. The elongated aperture with a smooth outer lip ends in a siphonal opening. The columellar lip is folded into several ridges.

On rocks and under stones, at low tide level and in shallow water. Carnivorous, using a sting to poison its prey. Mediterranean.

Other small mitre-shells are also found in the Mediterranean. **Beer Barrel; Mediterranean Cone Shell;** small **whelks.** Turrids: similar in shape but with pronounced ribbing or beading, and a notch at the top of the aperture.

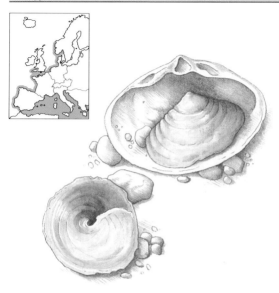

Round white shell with a thin curved shelf inside.

Low conical shell, very delicate and translucent when young, becoming thicker and opaque when mature. Surface slightly irregular when mature.

Filter feeders, locally common, living attached to rocks, small stones and shells on the lower shore and in shallow water. Often washed up in large quantities on the beach. Mediterranean, Atlantic, Channel and North Sea.

Do not mistake this for one half of a bivalve shell; **White Tortoiseshell Limpet.**

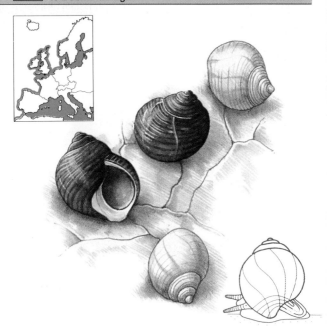

Grey-brown, black or reddish, with a sharply pointed apex and spirally banded with darker lines. White lip to aperture, inside brown. Outer lip meets body roughly parallel to spire.

Solid shell with rounded whorls, and a round turned-out aperture with no umbilicus or siphonal groove. Living animals can be distinguished from other winkles by the dark cross-bands on the tentacles. Edible.

On rocks, stones and seaweeds on the middle and lower intertidal zones of rocky shores, and in estuaries, feeding on plant debris and algae. Common throughout the area.

Flat Periwinkle; Rough Periwinkle; Small Periwinkle; Dog Whelk: siphonal groove at aperture; **Thick Top Shell.**

Grey or greenish conical shell decorated with purple zig-zags. Apex shows pearly yellow when worn. Aperture has a distinct rounded tooth on inner edge.

Thick shell with around 6 poorly defined whorls, a flat pearly base and mother-of-pearl interior. This top shell has an umbilicus which is often difficult to see in older shells.

On bare rocks and boulders, between high tide and middle shore, feeding on plant debris and algal particles. Atlantic north to Northern Ireland and western Channel.

***Monodonta turbinata*; *Gibbula* species and other top shells; Edible Periwinkle.**

29

Very symmetrical conical shell with straight sides and pointed apex. Yellow or pinkish background with darker red streaks.

Solid flat-bottomed shell of up to 12 ridged whorls, the largest of the European top shells. No umbilicus. There is also a white form.

On rocks and stones on the lower shore and below to a depth of around 100m:330ft. Mediterranean, Atlantic, Channel and North Sea.

None.

A brownish mottled rounded shell with aperture approximately the same size as body whorl, narrowing towards one end. Interior and edges of aperture white.

A thin rather fragile shell. The large body whorl almost encloses the spire which appears only as a small hole at the apex. In life the mantle partly covers the shell and the body (to 6cm:2⅜in long) cannot be entirely withdrawn into shell.

On a sandy or muddy bottom on the lower shore and in shallow water amongst seaweeds, on which this sea-slug feeds. Mediterranean.

Beer Barrel; Canoe Shell; cowries.

Whitish, mottled purple or brown. Long aperture with a thickened toothed outer lip curving in halfway down. Fine spiral ridging at base, fading out in centre of body whorl.

Solid, mainly smooth shell with a bulbous body whorl and pointed spire. Aperture opens by a short broad siphonal groove. No umbilicus.

On rocks on lower shore and beyond. Carnivorous. Mediterranean and adjacent parts of the Atlantic.

Pyrene scripta; **Mitre-shell**; small **whelks.**

Distinctively coloured snail-like shell with a rather flattened spire and large globe-shaped body whorl with an angular profile. Pale blue at spire shades to violet at base.

Thin, fragile, smooth shell with around 5 whorls. Aperture has a wavy edge.

Found washed up on Atlantic coasts after westerly gales. It lives on the surface of the ocean, floating under a raft of trapped air bubbles.

Several other violet sea snails may occasionally be found washed up, such as the **Small Violet Sea Snail** with fine V-shaped markings on shell and a more pointed spire.

Highly polished rounded shell of around 5 whorls covered with dark brown dots on a lighter background. Large umbilicus is partly obscured by a thin buttress projecting from columella.

Solid globe-shaped shell with a flattened spire and large aperture, closed in the living animal by an ear-shaped operculum. Eggs are laid on the sand embedded in a collar-shaped mass of sandy jelly.

On sandy shores, at and below low tide level, burrowing into sand and preying on bivalves, boring through their shells. Mediterranean.

Other **necklace shells** are found in the Mediterranean and elsewhere, similar in shape and structure but differing in colour and markings. **Large Necklace Shell** and **Common Necklace Shell**: slightly more pointed spires.

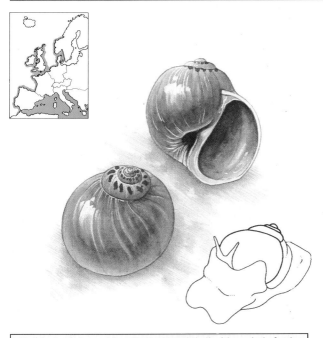

Polished pale brownish-yellow rounded shell with a spiral of red-brown spots following the sutures of spire. Large umbilicus.

Solid globe-shaped shell of 7 whorls with a short spire and large aperture, closed in the living animal by an ear-shaped operculum. Eggs are laid on the sand embedded in a collar-shaped mass of sandy jelly (see Necklace Shell).

On sandy shores, at and below low tide level, burrowing into sand and preying on bivalves, boring through their shells. Mediterranean, Atlantic, Channel and North Sea (rare).

Other **necklace shells** are found in the Mediterranean and elsewhere, similar in shape and structure but differing in colour and surface markings.

Very thick shell, grey and heavily ridged or smoother and often pure white. Yellow, black, pink or banded forms may also be found.

Thick heavy shell with around 5 whorls, the last being the largest, and a pointed spire. Aperture large with a deep groove where the siphon of the animal emerges. Interior of shell is like porcelain, not iridescent.

On rocks from high water down, feeding on barnacles, which it prises open, and mussels, whose shells it neatly drills through. The distinctive egg cases are often also found. Atlantic, Channel and North Sea.

Periwinkles: lack siphonal groove; **Common Northern Whelk:** much larger, thinner shell; **Netted Dog Whelk.**

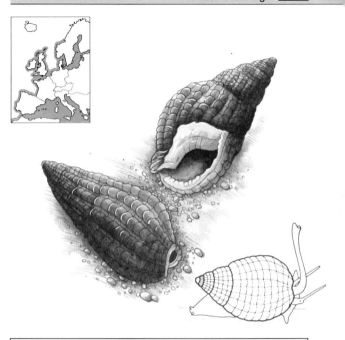

Brownish pointed shell with around 7 well-defined whorls, completely covered with longitudinal regularly beaded ribs. Aperture white with teeth on inner margin of outer lip.

Solid shell with a white interior and flared white edge to inner lip. Aperture has a groove at lower end where the animal's siphon emerges.

Burrows into sand or gravel, emerging to scavenge on dead crabs and other shellfish, probing inside their shells with its long proboscis. Found often in rather muddy places, on the lower shore and in shallow water. Throughout the area.

Dog Whelk; Thick-lipped Dog Whelk; Common Northern Whelk.

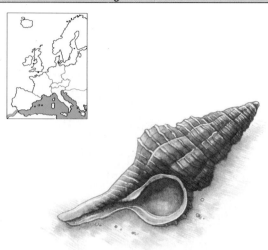

Pale yellowish- or reddish-brown shell with small oval aperture leading to a very long siphonal canal which remains open. High pointed spire of up to 9 whorls.

Solid spindle-shaped shell. Wide longitudinal ribs on spire and upper part of body whorl are crossed by numerous strong spiral ridges.

On sandy or muddy seabed in shallow to deeper water. Carnivorous. Mediterranean.

Sting Winkle; Murexes; Netted Dog Whelk.

Handsomely sculptured shell with sharp-edged longitudinal ribs crossed by numerous spiral ridges. Banded dark and lighter brown. Aperture white and thick-lipped.

A strong heavy shell, broadly oval in outline, the upper edge of aperture projecting slightly beyond body whorl. Short pointed spire. Inner edge of aperture has two folds, and the outer edge is slightly fluted.

In sand in shallow water, in the Mediterranean and off the West African coast. Rather rare.

None.

A distinctively shaped greyish shell with a high turreted spire, and the outer lip of columella expanded into 3 wide projections resembling a pelican's foot.

Elongated shell with a long siphonal canal forming a 4th 'finger'. The angular whorls of the spire are heavily ornamented with spiral beading and rows of conspicuous knobs.

Quite common, burrowing in mud or sand in shallow and moderately deep (to 80m:260ft) water. Usually found as empty shells washed up on the beach. Throughout the area.

None when mature although the extended lip is not so pronounced in younger shells.

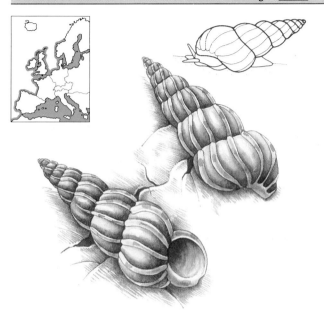

Narrow high-spired shell whose rounded whorls each bear around 9 strong ribs, connecting with those on adjacent whorls at the sutures. White to reddish-brown.

Strong tapering shell, with numerous deeply separated whorls, smooth except for the ribs. Aperture round with a thick lip. In life the aperture is sealed with a horny operculum. The snail has a long proboscis.

In shallow water down to 80m:260ft, occasionally found on extreme lower shore on rocks near sand or mud. Throughout the area, generally found as empty shells washed up on the beach.

Tower Shell; Common Cerith.

COMMON CERITH

◆ to **4·5cm:1¾in** high   *Cerithium vulgatum*

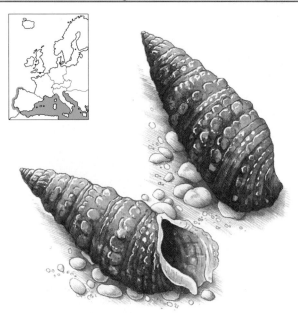

Heavily sculptured shell, the numerous angular whorls bearing spiral beading and rows of knobs. Small oval aperture has a notch in upper edge and opens by a short siphonal groove.

Narrow, elongated shell with a pointed spire. Outer edge of aperture has a slightly frilled edge. Covered with a dark brown velvety periostracum in life.

In shallow water, on a sandy, stony or muddy bottom, down to around 10m:33ft. Quite common in the Mediterranean, rarer on adjacent Atlantic coasts.

Tower Shell; Common Wentletrap.

ITALIAN KEYHOLE LIMPET

Diodora italica   to **4·5cm:1¾in** across

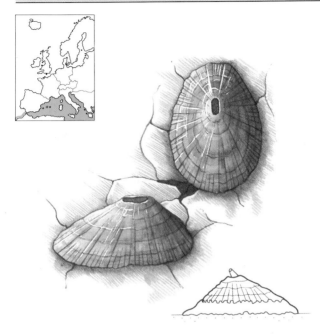

Grey-white oval shell with oblong hole at apex. Distinct ridges radiate from apex. Sometimes banded bluish or grey.

Strong conical shell. Interior white. In the living shell a short siphon protrudes from the hole at apex.

On rocks on lower shore and in shallow water to 10m:33ft, browsing on algae. Mediterranean.

The very similar **Keyhole Limpet** is found on Atlantic, Channel and North Sea coasts; **Common Limpet.**

Fragments of shells, small bivalve shells and small stones are attached to the upper surface of this shell, in a spiral which follows whorl formation. Base free of attachments.

Under the attachments this is a rather flattened creamy or fawn coloured top-shaped shell with a wavy-edged base. Rows of small bumps radiate from centre of base. Looks like a moving pile of debris when alive.

In shallow water, feeding on detritus. Mediterranean.

None.

Glossy fawn-brown shell with a long slit-like aperture underneath.
Two dark spots above each end of aperture. The back is crossed
by 2 paler bands.

Smooth rather lightweight oval shell with a white base and
interior. Both lips of aperture are toothed. The ends of the
aperture are tinged red.

Rare shell of deeper water, found in the Mediterranean and in the
eastern Atlantic north to the Azores.

Pear Cowrie; European Yellow Cowrie.

Handsome glossy orange-brown shell with white slit-like aperture along base. Back of shell mottled darker brown, with 3 indistinct bands of darker shading.

Solid smooth pear-shaped shell with wide margins. Both lips of aperture toothed. Interior white.

A rare shell of deeper water over a rocky bottom, associated with seaweed, in the Mediterranean and off the Atlantic coast north to Portugal.

Lurid Cowrie: duller in colour, narrow margin, two dark spots at either end; **Yellow European Cowrie:** thinner margins, yellower in colour.

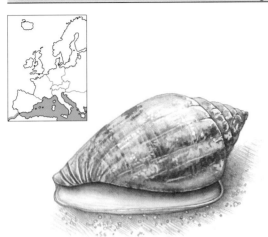

Shiny olive- or yellowish-green shell with brown markings and usually lighter banding. Aperture long and narrow with smooth edges and opening at base by a short siphonal canal.

Smooth conical shell with a large body whorl with a distinct shoulder, and a short compressed spire. The living animal has a poisonous sting which can be painful and irritating.

In sand in shallow water. It is carnivorous, capturing its prey with a hollow venomous tooth, feeding on worms and gastropods. Mediterranean.

Beer Barrel; Striate Bubble.

ROUGH STAR-SHELL

to **5cm:2in** high   *Astraea (Turbo) rugosa*

Reddish-brown heavily ornamented shell with scarlet area at base alongside the silvery aperture. In life the aperture is closed by an orange operculum with spiral markings.

Squat solid heavy shell of around 7 whorls each with a row of rounded bumps on their upper surface and spiny ridges on the side. Interior silvery.

A rather rare shell of rocky shores, from low tide level downwards. Mediterranean and the Atlantic coasts of Spain and Portugal.

None.

BONNET LIMPET

Capulus hungaricus   to **5cm:2in** across

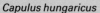

Pale yellowish or brownish, sometimes marked reddish, with a pronounced downcurved apex. Most of shell except apex covered with a brown horny periostracum.

Shell shaped like a 'liberty cap' with periostracum forming a fringe around base. Interior white. Fine ridges run radially from apex and the shell is usually marked with distinct growth lines.

Attached to rocks, and to oysters and scallops. Occasionally found at the lowest levels of rocky shores but usually in water to 100m:330ft. Mediterranean, Channel, Atlantic, North Sea.

Do not mistake the empty shell for one half of a bivalve shell such as a cockle; **Slipper Limpet.**

A boat-shaped shell, arched and with a low coiled apex bent to one side. Inside, a white shelf extends from the apex about half the length of the shell.

The ridged surface of this robust shell is yellowish- or pinkish-white, mottled and streaked brown and purple. The interior is shiny white marked with brown. Lives stacked up in piles of up to 12, youngest individuals at the top.

In shallow water, attached to other slipper limpets or to bivalves. A pest in oyster beds, smothering the oysters. Introduced from America, now found on Channel, North Sea and Atlantic coasts.

Bonnet Limpet.

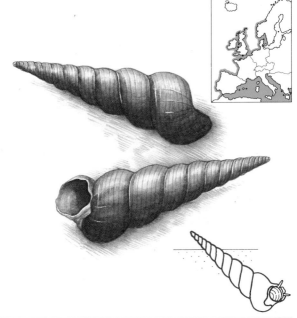

Narrow conical shell of up to 19 distinct spirally ridged whorls. Small circular aperture. Pinkish-brown to yellowish.

Solid elongated shell tapering to a pointed apex. Aperture has a smooth edge and no siphonal canal.

In shallow waters to depths of 80m:260ft, burrowing into sand or mud. It is a filter feeder, filtering off food particles drawn into the shell with water. Throughout the area.

A close relative with straighter sides and less distinct whorls is found in the Mediterranean only. **Needle Shell:** much smaller; **Common Cerith:** knobbed ornament.

51

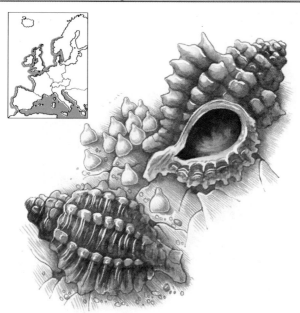

Heavily and unevenly sculptured yellowish-white shell with siphonal canal enclosed to form a tube when mature. Oval aperture with a thickened, toothed outer lip.

Solid thick-walled shell with a pointed spire of around 5 turret-like heavily ridged whorls, and a large body whorl. Wide longitudinal ribs are crossed by strong spiral ridges. Vase-shaped egg capsules similar to those of Dog Whelk.

On muddy gravel or sandy bottom, from low tide and beyond into deep water, preying on oysters whose shells it drills through. Throughout the area.

Common Northern Whelk; Dog Whelk; Netted Dog Whelk; Spindle Shell; Murexes. The accidentally introduced Oyster Drill (*Urosalpinx cinerea*) from North America is very similar but smoother and its siphonal canal never closes.

Curved oval shell with a large aperture tapering towards the sunken apex. A yellowish-brown periostracum covers most of exterior except for a white margin.

Thin, quite strong shell with fine lines on surface. Interior white. The living animal (a sea-slug) is longer than the shell and cannot completely withdraw into it.

Lives in sand or mud in shallow water. Mediterranean and Atlantic coasts north to the Channel.

Striate Bubble.

53

to **7cm:2¾in** across (usually smaller)   *Patella vulgata*

Tall conical shell, thick ribs running from apex to base. Colour variable, yellowish-brown, greenish-blue or greyish, with horizontal banding. Interior creamy or yellowish, shiny.

The commonest of several rather similar limpets found on European shores. The head scar inside the apex of shell is brown or white, and the tiny tentacles around the edge of the living animal are transparent in this species.

On rocks on upper and middle shore, impossible to dislodge when exposed, moving around and browsing on seaweeds when submerged. Very common, Atlantic, Channel, North Sea.

Mediterranean Limpet: Mediterranean only; **Keyhole Limpets; Tortoiseshell Limpet.**

54

Brownish oval shell with a row of holes along one edge. Shell patchily covered with a brownish or greenish periostracum. Mother of pearl interior.

Strong shell with a flattened coiled apex. Surface ridged and corrugated. Holes towards the apical end of shell are closed. Edible.

Among rocks and under stones in shallow water, browsing on algae. Mediterranean and coasts north to the Channel Islands.

Common Ormer: shell more heavily corrugated and often encrusted with lime from growth of calcareous algae, Mediterranean only.

DYE MUREX

to **8cm:3⅛in** high *Murex (Bolinus) brandaris*

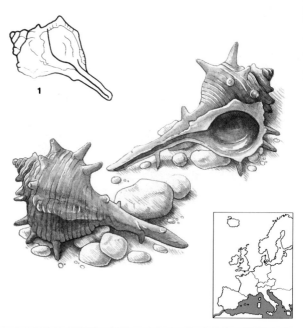

Yellowish-grey shell of around 6 whorls with a long siphonal canal making up around half the total length. Stout spines on the body whorl and siphonal canal.

Solid shell with a large rounded body whorl and a short pointed spire. Some forms have much shorter blunt spines (**1**). Interior of aperture darker brownish-yellow. The Romans made the Imperial Purple dye from this animal.

On muddy and stony bottoms, in shallow water. Carnivorous, feeding on bivalves. Mediterranean and the West African Coast.

Murex; Whelks; Sting Winkle.

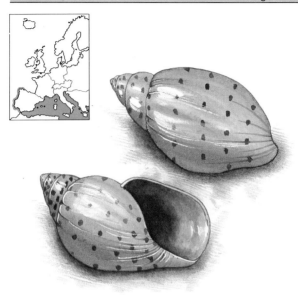

Pale orange-brown shell with spiral bands of darker squarish dots and dashes. No folds on columella.

Thin smooth rounded glossy shell with a large body whorl and a short conical spire of up to 3 well-defined rounded whorls. Large slightly elongated aperture with smooth outer edge. Interior brown.

A deeper water shell, living in sand at depths of 50–300m: 165–1000ft. Carnivorous, feeding on molluscs and other small animals. Atlantic, off West Africa and Spanish and Portuguese coasts.

None in the region.

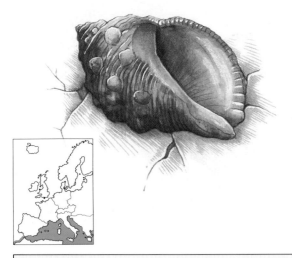

Brown, knobby, helmet-shaped shell with a large orange or pink aperture and columella.

Solid shell with a short blunt conical spire of several angular whorls and a large body whorl. Body whorl decorated with 4 spiral rows of knobs. Inside of outer lip of aperture ridged. Colour varies from light grey to red-brown.

A carnivore, feeding especially on mussels, and living in the intertidal zone on rocky shores in the Mediterranean and West Africa.

Rough Star-shell; Knobbed Helmet Shell.

COMMON NORTHERN WHELK

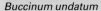

Buccinum undatum   to **10cm:4in** high

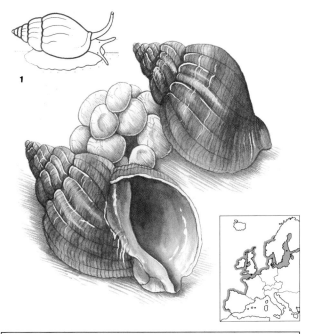

1

Pale yellowish-brown shell, with 7–8 well-defined ribbed and corded whorls, empty shells often bearing traces of the darker horny periostracum.

Strong shell, the walls relatively thinner than in smaller whelks. Large body whorl and conical pointed spire. Aperture large with a short siphonal canal. Columella and interior white tinged orange. Egg cases laid in a large mass (**1**).

Common on sandy or muddy shores from the lower shore down to around 100m:330ft. Empty shells are often inhabited by hermit crabs. Atlantic, Channel, North Sea and western Baltic.

Dog Whelk; Sting Winkle; other **whelks.**

KNOBBED HELMET SHELL
to **11cm:4¼in** high   *Cassidaria echinophora*

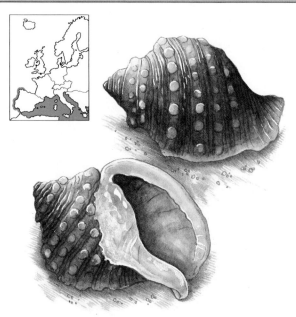

Pale yellow-brown shell with raised spiral white-knobbed bands on a smooth surface. Aperture and columella white, columella expanded in a thin layer attached to body of shell.

Solid shell with globular body whorl and conical spire of knobbed whorls. Aperture large and elongated, opening by a short siphonal canal. Outer lip of aperture blunt-toothed on inside edge. Edible.

A shell of shallow water, living on sand at depths of up to 10m:33ft and preying on sea urchins. Caught and sold in fish markets. Mediterranean and adjacent Atlantic coasts.

Several related species lacking the knobbed ornament also live at greater depths in the Mediterranean and adjacent Atlantic; **Giant Tun.**

OLLA VOLUTE

Cymbium olla   to **13cm:5in** high

Large pinky-beige shell with a deep suture separating the high-shouldered body whorl from the short knob-like spire. Aperture and columella lighter in colour.

Thin lightweight oval to oblong shell. Smooth glossy surface is sometimes roughened by sand grains trapped under the glaze. Large wide aperture with smooth outer lip and several folds on columella has a broad siphonal notch at base.

A carnivore, preying on sea urchins, it lives at depths of 50–100m:165–330ft in sand off the coasts of Portugal, Spain and North Africa (Morocco).

None in the region.

GIANT WORM SHELL
tube to **20cm:8in** long   *Vermetus gigas*

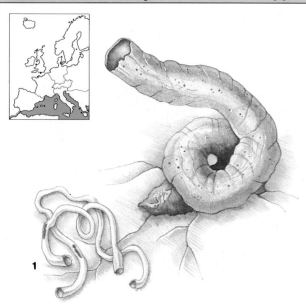

1

Unusual relative of the turret shells and ceriths in which the typical gastropod shell appears to have been 'unrolled' to form a coiled greyish tube.

One of several similar worm shells which are found free or attached to stones or shells. The living animal is not a worm but a mollusc.

Mediterranean only, on sand or attached to rocks, stones or shells. This animal is a filter feeder, filtering out food particles from water drawn into the shell.

Do not mistake for the limy tubes of various polychaete worms (tube worms) (**1**) which are common throughout the area, on stones, rocks and seaweed. A Worm Shell tube always starts as a spiral, even if further growth is irregular.

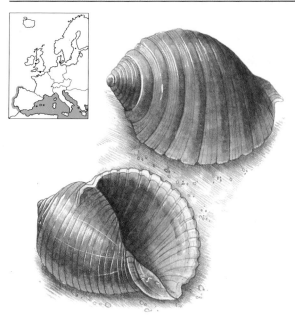

Large rounded brownish-yellow shell with alternating thick and thin spiral ridges. Large white aperture has a fluted white outer lip. Deep suture between body whorl and spire.

Rather thin-walled shell with a large rounded body whorl and a short spire of up to 7 whorls. Columella much twisted. Aperture opens by a short siphonal canal. Interior white.

A deep water shell, found off the Atlantic coast of Spain and Portugal and West Africa and the adjacent Mediterranean.

Knobbed Helmet Shell; Rock Shell.

Whitish shell with red-brown markings, with spiral ridges and bands of blunt knobs. Thick rounded ridges (varices) run down each whorl, spaced about two-thirds of a whorl apart.

Large solid shell with high pointed spire. The large aperture has a flared scalloped outer lip and a siphonal canal. Columella and interior of aperture white, with brown markings on ridges of outer lip. Brown blotch at base of columella.

On sandy or rocky seabed in shallow to deeper water. Carnivorous, preying on other molluscs and sea urchins. Mediterranean and adjacent Atlantic.

Parthenope's Triton; Triton.

OTHER SMALL GASTROPODS

Small Periwinkle (1)
5mm:³⁄₁₆in. Top of exposed
rocky shores, in crevices. T (ex.
Balt.). *Alvania cancellata* (2)
3mm:⅛in. Lower shore and
shallow water, amongst rocks
and gravel. T. **Looping Snail (3)**
3mm:⅛in. Muddy upper shore,
amongst seaweed and stones.
Med., Atl. *Paludestrina
jenkinsii* (4) 5mm:³⁄₁₆in. In
mud, in brackish water. Atl.,
Ch., N Sea, Balt. **Laver Spire
Shell (5)** 6mm:¼in. On mud in
estuaries & in brackish water. T
(ex. Med.). **Margin Shell (6)**
7mm:¼in. On stony and sandy
bottoms. Med. *Otina ovata* (7)
5mm:³⁄₁₆in. Upper shore, in
crevices and empty barnacle
shells. Atl., Ch. **Small Risso (8)**
7mm:¼in. Lower shore and
shallow water, under stones and
seaweeds. Atl., Ch., N Sea, Balt.
Clanculus corallinus (9)
7mm:¼in. On rocks, shallow
water. Med.

OTHER GASTROPODS

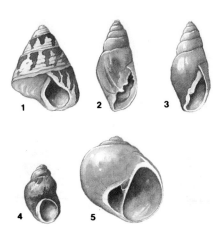

Grooved Top Shell (1)
1cm:⅜in. On sand or mud,
lower tide level to 100m:330ft.
Med., Atl., Ch. *Phytia myosotis*
(2) 9mm:⅜in. Estuaries, saltmarshes, under stones. Med.,
Atl., Ch. *Leucophytia
bidentata* **(3)** 9mm:⅜in.
Saltmarshes, upper shore, in
crevices and amongst debris.
Med., Atl., Ch. **Pheasant Shell
(4)** 8mm:⁵⁄₁₆in. Rock pools,
lower shore. Med., Atl., Ch.
Common Necklace Shell (5)
2cm:¾in. In sand, lower shore
and below. T (ex. Balt.). **Small
Violet Sea Snail (6)** 1.5cm:⅝in.
Open ocean, washed up after
storms. Atl. **Northern Cowrie
(7)** 1cm:⅜in. On rocks, shallow
water and below. Atl., Ch., N
Sea. **False Simnia (8)** 2cm:¾in.
Deep water. Med.

White Tortoiseshell Limpet (1)
1·25cm:½in. Lower shore, with
kelp. T. *Pisania striata* (2)
1·5cm:⅝in. Rocks, shallow
water. Med. & adjacent Atl.
Tritonalia aciculata (3)
2cm:¾in. Rocks & sand,
shallow water and beyond. Med.
& adjacent Atl. *Pyrene scripta*
(4) 2cm:¾in. Rocks, shallow
water. Med. *Gibbula magus* (5)
1·5cm:⅝in. In sand, shallow
water. Med., At., Ch. *Gibbula
divaricata* (6) 2cm:¾in. Lower
shore & beyond, under stones &
seaweed. Med. *Monodonta
turbinata* (7) 2·5cm:1in. Rocks,
lower shore. Med. **European
Yellow Cowrie (8)** 3cm:1¼in.
Deep water. Med., Atl. ·

OTHER GASTROPODS

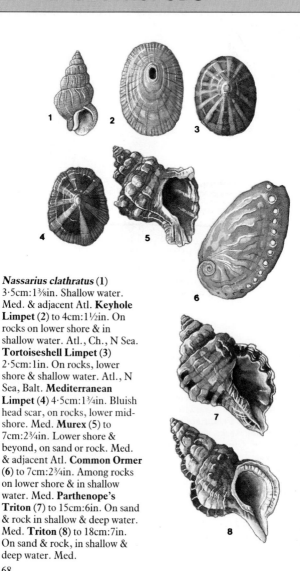

Nassarius clathratus (**1**)
3·5cm:1⅜in. Shallow water.
Med. & adjacent Atl. **Keyhole
Limpet** (**2**) to 4cm:1½in. On
rocks on lower shore & in
shallow water. Atl., Ch., N Sea.
Tortoiseshell Limpet (**3**)
2·5cm:1in. On rocks, lower
shore & shallow water. Atl., N
Sea, Balt. **Mediterranean
Limpet** (**4**) 4·5cm:1¾in. Bluish
head scar, on rocks, lower mid-
shore. Med. **Murex** (**5**) to
7cm:2¾in. Lower shore &
beyond, on sand or rock. Med.
& adjacent Atl. **Common Ormer**
(**6**) to 7cm:2¾in. Among rocks
on lower shore & in shallow
water. Med. **Parthenope's
Triton** (**7**) to 15cm:6in. On sand
& rock in shallow & deep water.
Med. **Triton** (**8**) to 18cm:7in.
On sand & rock, in shallow &
deep water. Med.

Small rounded-triangular shell hinged with interlocking rows of numerous similar teeth on each valve. Brownish, with a yellowish periostracum and a mother-of-pearl interior.

Small smooth shell with identical valves and a finely scalloped edge. The interior bears two equal adductor muscle scars and no pallial sinus. The surface is scored with fine concentric lines. The living animal has no siphons.

Burrows in sand, mud or gravel. In shallow water and to depths of 100m:330ft. Throughout the area.

One of several species of nut-shells in the area. Some are white or yellowish and have one end more elongated. They are distinguished from other small bivalves by the rows of similar teeth.

LITTLE COCKLE
to 1·25cm: ½in long

Cardium exiguum

Dull brownish shell with around 20 flattened ribs and a whitish interior. Ribs show tubercles only towards the front edge of shell when mature.

Arched shell with similar valves, rounded beaks and ribs running down to a serrated edge. Hinge region on each valve has a central tooth flanked by elongated teeth on either side. Adductor muscle scars equal, no pallial sinus.

Below low tide line down to depths of 60m:200ft, just under the surface in sand and mud. Empty shells commonly found on the beach. Throughout the area (except Baltic).

C. papillosum: Mediterranean and Atlantic coasts only, has white interior tinged pink and all the ribs carry tubercles.

Delicate glossy shells, translucent white tinged pink, yellow or violet, with fine concentric lines on outer surface. Empty shells often still held together by the strong ligament.

Flat thin fragile shells, with smooth edges. Slightly more pointed at one end (the posterior end), with beak placed slightly off-centre, towards the posterior. Equal adductor muscle scars and pallial sinus present on interior.

In clean fine sand, burrowing under the surface. Middle shore to low tide level and below. A filter-feeder, extending its 2 siphons above sand to feed. Throughout, often abundant.

***Tellina fabula*; Distorted Tellin; Faroe Sunset Shell; Common Nut-shell; Banded Wedge Shell.**

71

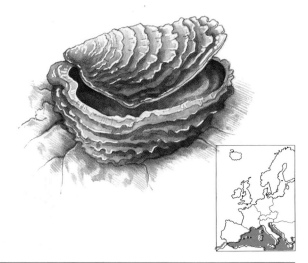

Round whitish to yellowish shell with pinkish beaks. Lower (left) valve shaped like a cup and attached to rock, upper (right) valve forming a lid. Interior brownish tinged violet.

Solid shell with a ridged and knobbed surface. An insignificant member of a group of shells whose tropical representatives are very decorative, the surfaces often covered with large leaf-like projections.

Attached to rocks in shallow water and beyond. Mediterranean, rare.

Pseudochama gryphina (Mediterranean): larger (to 4cm:1½in), surface covered with small vertical plates, interior yellow to greenish. Attached to rock by a cup-shaped *right* valve, the *left* valve forming the lid.

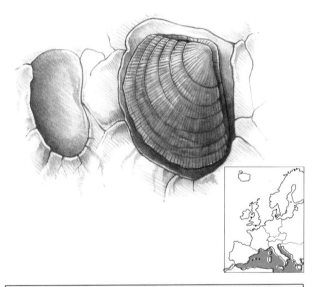

Greyish-white rather irregularly shaped shell with ridged surface and radiating ribs on exterior. Smooth margin on interior.

Solid shell rounded-triangular in outline, longer than broad with rounded beak set towards the front end. Two central teeth in each valve. Fine concentric markings on exterior of valves.

The living animal bores into rock and mud. Found in shallow water. Mediterranean.

Empty shells washed up on the beach could be mistaken for various species, such as small cockles, wedge-shells etc. ***Notirus irus***: surface with overlapping concentric ridges, lives in rock crevices.

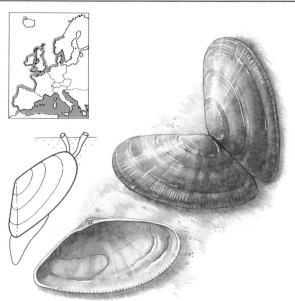

Highly polished brightly coloured shell with fine radiating grooves. Colours vary from yellow through greenish-brown to violet. Interior usually marked violet.

Flattened elongated shell, unlike most other wedge-shells elongated at the front end. Margin serrated on the inside. Equal adductor muscle scars and pallial sinus on interior.

Quite common on exposed sandy shores from the middle of the shore to water 20m:65ft deep, burrowing in sand. Throughout the area (except Baltic).

Tellins; Faroe Sunset Shell.

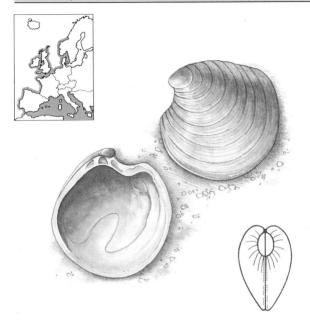

Round shell with a small rounded curved beak and a smooth surface marked by concentric growth lines. Smooth edges to valves. White or yellowish. Interior white.

Solid rounded shell whose beaks curve forward to border a small heart-shaped depression (best seen on a closed whole shell). Three central teeth in each valve. Equal adductor muscle scars and pallial sinus present on interior.

Common on sandy shores around very low tide level and down to depths of 125m:400ft. Burrows in sand or shell gravel using its strong foot and taking in water from above the surface by its double siphon. Throughout the area (except Baltic).

Rayed Artemis; Northern Lucina; Striped Venus; Banded Venus.

Almost round chalky white shell, slightly longer than broad, with a small curved beak. Surface finely ridged. Anterior adductor muscle scar elongated. No pallial sinus.

Solid rounded shell with similar valves and forward facing beaks. Hinge of 2 central teeth and elongated plate-like teeth behind them. Brown periostracum which seldom persists. Interior white. The live animal has a very long foot.

Burrows into muddy sand or gravel at low tide level and beyond. Throughout the area (except Baltic).

Round Double-tooth: up to 2·5cm:1in, slightly broader than long; **Rayed Artemis** and other **venus shells:** pallial sinus on interior; *Astarte* species: different type of hinge region.

THICK TROUGH SHELL

Spisula solida

to **4·5cm**:1¾in long

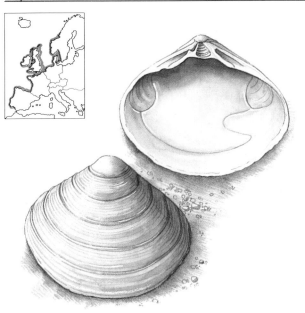

Heavy chalky white shell with smooth concentric grooves on surface. Slightly longer than broad. Interior white.

Symmetrical triangular-oval shell with equal valves. Small forward-facing beak. The sides of the lateral teeth have fine vertical lines. Equal adductor muscle scars and pallial sinus present on interior.

Common in sand and shell on the extreme lower shore to water 100m:330ft deep. Shells often washed up on shore in large numbers. Atlantic, Channel and North Sea.

Cut Trough Shell (*S. subtruncata*): broader than long, more angular in outline; Elliptical Trough Shell (*S. elliptica*): more delicate, nearly smooth, longer than broad; **Rayed Trough Shell.**

to **4·5cm:1¾in** long   *Venus striatula*

Creamy white to yellowish shell with brown markings, surface covered with irregular, quite fine concentric ridges. Colour tends to be concentrated in several wide rays.

Solid rounded-triangular shell with similar valves, with small forward-curving beaks. Internal edge of valves serrated. Three central teeth in each valve. Equal adductor muscle scars and pallial sinus on interior.

Common in sandy bays, burrowing in sand with the aid of its large strong foot. From the lower shore down to depths of 50m:165ft. Throughout the area (except Baltic).

Rayed Artemis; Banded Venus; other **venus shells.**

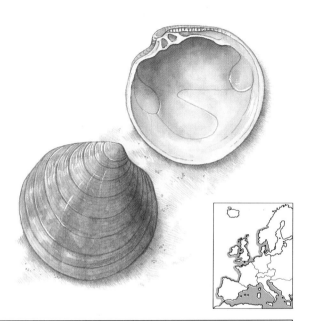

Round shell with small curved beak and surface marked with smooth concentric ridges. Pale brownish, often with darker bands radiating from the beak. Interior white.

Solid shell whose beaks curve forward to border a small heart-shaped depression (best seen on a closed whole shell). Three central teeth in each valve. Equal adductor muscle scars and pallial sinus on interior. Smooth edges to valves.

On sandy shores, on the lower shore and below, burrowing under the surface with its strong foot, feeding by means of its double siphon projecting above the surface. Mediterranean, Atlantic, Channel and North Sea.

Smooth Artemis; smaller, smoother surface; **Striped Venus; Banded Venus; Northern Lucina.**

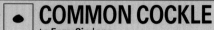

COMMON COCKLE
to **5cm:2in** long

Cardium edule

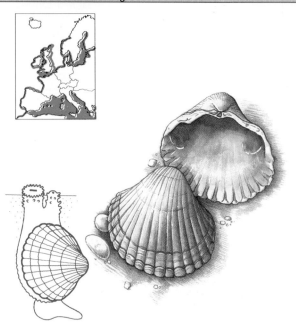

Off-white or brownish, with a rounded beak, serrated edge, and some 25 rounded ridged ribs on exterior, corresponding flat ribs running a short way in from edge on inside.

Solid rounded-triangular shell, the two halves similar. Adductor muscle scars equal and no pallial sinus on interior. Hinge composed of 2 central teeth flanked by elongated ridges. Interior whitish with brown marks. Edible.

On sandy or muddy beaches and estuaries, just below the surface, from the middle shore and beyond. Throughout the area, locally abundant, farmed commercially in some places.

Spiny Cockle; Prickly Cockle; Lagoon Cockle; Little Cockle; Egg Cockle.

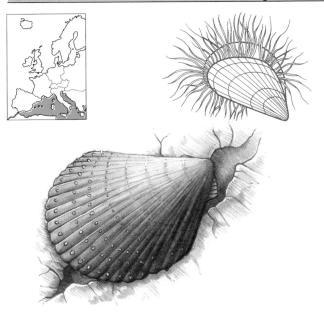

Asymmetrical oval white shell, dirty brown when mature, broader than long, with around 20 radial ribs bearing short spines. Serrated edge.

Rather flattened shell resembling a scallop. Anterior 'ear' larger than posterior. Valves similar. No teeth on the hinge region in mature shells. The living animal swims with the aid of long tentacles which cannot be retracted into the shell.

In rock crevices and under stones, in shallow water. Mediterranean (also found in the Caribbean and SE coast of the United States).

Scallops: shells generally more symmetrical and the 'ears' are larger and more distinct; **Gaping File-shell:** smaller, 50 spiny ribs, the closed shell shows distinct gape between valves at anterior end.

81

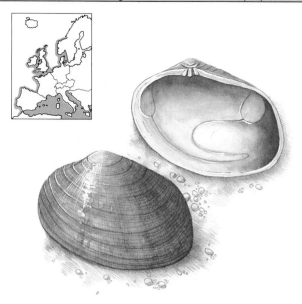

Rather oblong blunt-ended shell, with fine radial lines crossed by concentric ridges. Yellowish-grey with indistinct purple markings. White interior often marked with violet.

Solid shell with similar valves, the small curved forward-facing beak set well towards the front end. Hinge has 3 small central teeth on each valve. Equal adductor muscle scars and pallial sinus on interior.

Very common, burrowing in sand or gravel from very low tide level down to depths of around 180m:600ft. Throughout the area (except Baltic).

Cross-cut Carpet Shell; Golden Carpet Shell: edible, golden interior to a greyish shell; **Banded Carpet Shell:** concentric but no radial lines.

Lightweight thin pale shell with a glossy surface, tinged violet with brownish rays running from the beak to edge. Also marked with concentric banding. Interior tinged violet.

Smooth solid triangular-oval shell, with equal valves, often bearing remains of a thin light brown shiny periostracum. Hinge region has central and lateral teeth. Small forward-facing beak. Pallial sinus present on interior.

Common in sand or shell gravel, into which they burrow, from the extreme lower shore to depths of 10m:330ft. Empty shells often washed up on shore. Throughout area (except Baltic).

The colouring of this shell varies somewhat throughout the region, some forms having a white interior. Other trough shells e.g. **Thick Trough Shell**: edges of teeth in hinge are milled; **Tellins.**

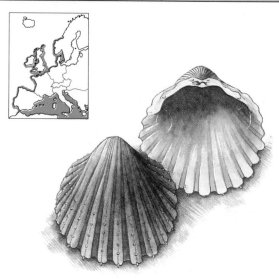

Off-white to brownish shell with a rounded beak and around 18 well-spaced ribs on each valve. Ribs carry small spines mostly at front and at edges of shell.

Heavy arched shell, rounded-triangular in outline with a serrated edge. Ribs tend to fade out towards the beak. Interior white, with flat ribs running some way in from edge. Equal adductor muscle scars and no pallial sinus on interior.

Burrows just under the surface of sand, in shallow water and beyond. Empty shells generally found washed up on the beach. Throughout the area (except Baltic).

C. tuberculatum: larger, ribs knobbed, not spiny; **Spiny Cockle**: to 10cm:4in long, more ribs with more prominent spines.

Heavy shell with many prominent concentric ridges crossed by radial ribs. Reddish-fawn with purplish markings.

Rather oblong with a blunt rear end. Valves equal, the small curved forward-facing beaks set well towards the front end. Hinge has 3 small central teeth on each valve. Equal adductor muscle scars and pallial sinus on interior.

Burrowing in sand or muddy gravel on the lower shore. Mediterranean and Atlantic north to the Channel.

Pullet Carpet Shell: similar but less pronounced ornamentation; **Banded Carpet Shell:** concentric but no radiating lines; **Golden Carpet Shell:** golden interior to a greyish shell, small, edible.

COMMON SADDLE OYSTER
to **6cm:2⅜in** long   *Anomia ephippium*

White to pale brown shell with a deep rounded cleft at the anterior end of the flat lower valve through which the animal is attached to a substrate by strong threads (byssus).

Roughly circular shell with dissimilar valves, the upper thicker and slightly domed, the lower flat, thinner, translucent, conforming to the shape of substrate. Upper surface scaly, often encrusted. Pearly interior.

Common, attached to rocks and larger bivalves from middle shore down to shallow water. Usually found as separated valves washed up on beach. Throughout area (except Baltic).

Several saddle oysters are found in the region, such as the Ribbed Saddle Oyster (*Monia patelliformis*), to 2·5cm:1in diameter, with 20–30 ribs.

Venus verrucosa to **6cm:2⅜in** long

Greyish-white shell with brown markings, the surface covered with warty concentric ridges, more prominent towards the rear end.

Almost round heavy shell with rounded forward-facing beaks bordering a small heart-shaped area (best seen in a whole closed shell). Inside edge finely ridged. Interior white with brown markings. Three central teeth in hinge. Pallial sinus present.

Burrows into shell gravel or sand, from extreme lower shore to depths of 100m:330ft. Usually found as empty shells washed up on the beach. Mediterranean, Atlantic, Channel, North Sea.

Other **venus shells; Smooth Artemis** and **Rayed Artemis:** no ridges on inside of valve edge; *Astarte* species: no pallial sinus, hinge region different.

BLUNT TELLIN
to **6cm:2⅜in** long

Tellina crassa

Yellowish-white shell with an ochre periostracum and sometimes faint pink rays. Valves slightly unequal, left flatter than right. Numerous concentric ridges on surface.

Thick oval shell. Inside of edge smooth. Beaks set slightly towards rear of shell. Posterior adductor muscle scar shorter and thicker than anterior. Two central teeth and 2 lateral teeth in hinge. Pallial sinus present.

Common, burrowing in mud, coarse sand and shell gravel in shallow water down to depths of 150m:500ft. Atlantic, Channel and North Sea.

Trough shells; venus shells; Rayed Artemis; Large Sunset Shell; Peppery Furrow Shell.

LARGE SUNSET SHELL

Gari depressa | to **6cm:2⅜in** long

Yellowish-white with pinkish or lilac rays, and fine concentric lines and ridges. Greenish-brown periostracum often still adheres to empty shells at edges.

Solid oval shell with smooth edges and a gap between valves at the rear end. Interior white to purple. Hinge region has 1 or 2 small peg-like cardinal teeth and no lateral teeth. Pallial sinus present. Living animal has 2 short siphons.

Quite common, burrowing in sand on the extreme lower shore and beyond to water 50m:165ft deep. Mediterranean, Atlantic, Channel and North Sea. Usually found as empty shells on the beach.

Striped Solen; Sand Gaper and **Blunt Gaper:** generally larger and heavier, hinge region different; **Otter Shell:** hinge region different.

PEPPERY FURROW SHELL

to **6cm:2⅜in** long   *Scrobicularia plana*

Greyish to yellowish shell with concentrically ridged surface. Greyish-brown periostracum often still adhering to edges of empty shells. Interior white.

Lightweight oval flattened shell with similar valves. Hinge region has 2 central teeth on left valve, 1 on right. Posterior adductor muscle scar shorter than anterior. Pallial sinus present. Living animal has very long siphons. Edible.

Common between high and low tidemarks, burrowing in mud or muddy sand, often found in estuaries as it can stand very low salinities. Throughout the area.

Blunt Tellin: lives below low tide level, shell with more marked concentric ridges; **Thick Trough Shell:** heavier shell, hinge region has lateral teeth; **Sand Gaper:** different hinge region.

Chlamys varia   to **6cm:2⅜in** across (often smaller)

Finely ribbed oval shell with very unequal 'ears' on either side of the beak. Often brightly coloured, spotted and streaked.

Thin arched shell with serrated edge and around 28 ribs running from beak to edge. Hinge region has no teeth in mature shells. One central muscle scar on interior of valves. The animal swims by flapping the 2 valves open and shut.

Free-living or attached to rocks by strong threads (the byssus), on the extreme lower shore and beyond to depths of around 80m:260ft. Common. Throughout the area (except Baltic).

Queen Scallop; Tiger Scallop; Hunchback Scallop (*C. distorta*): irregular shell with around 70 fine ribs, the right valve becoming cemented to substrate.

White shell with brown zig-zag markings, sometimes rather smudged and indistinct.

Heavy smooth nearly round shell with ridged inside edge. Valves similar. It has a small beak and a curved hinge line with many small teeth.

Common, burrowing in sand, mud or shell gravel in shallow water and to water around 80m:260ft deep. Empty shells found washed up on the beach. Throughout the region.

Hairy Dog Cockle: (Mediterranean only): very similar but with a hairy periostracum, shell violet; true **cockles:** strongly ribbed and with a different arrangement of teeth in the hinge region.

Cigar-shaped yellowish shell, covered with a shiny brown periostracum. No teeth on hinge. Interior white.

Elongated shell with a toothless hinge near anterior end, and small beaks which do not touch. Surface finely lined. Edible.

Bores into limestone and coral with the aid of an acid secretion. Found in shallow water in the Mediterranean only.

Razor Shell; other **mussels.**

93

Unusual shaped shell with projections either side of hinge region, one of which is much longer than the other. Mother-of-pearl interior.

Asymmetrical flattened shell with slightly dissimilar valves. Smooth wavy edge. Surface with concentric overlapping ridges. The grey-brown exterior is covered with a brown periostracum in the living animal.

Attached to rocks and stones on seabed in shallow to deep water. Mediterranean and adjacent Atlantic.

Several related species.

Reddish-brown shell with darker markings, covered with a persistent glossy brown periostracum. Fine concentric growth lines. Interior whitish.

Heavy smooth rounded-triangular arched shell with prominent curved forward-facing beaks. Darker rays sometimes lead from beak to edge. Interior has equal adductor muscle scars and a pallial sinus. Hinge region resembles that of venus shells. Edible.

Burrowing in sand and gravel. Shallow water and to depths of 100m:330ft. Mediterranean and adjacent Atlantic.

Other **venus shells; gapers:** hinge region different.

95

Pinkish shell with 2 paler rays running from beak to lower edge. Coarse concentric growth lines on surface are crossed by diagonal wavy grooves. Interior white tinged pink.

Thin oblong shell with rounded ends and beaks set slightly forward. Valves gape at both ends. One central tooth on left valve, 2 on right. Adductor muscle scars unequal. Greenish-yellow horny periostracum.

Burrows in sand or shell gravel. Found on the extreme lower shore and beyond to water around 50m:165ft deep. Mediterranean, where it is quite common.

Razor shells; Gapers and **Otter shells:** different types of hinge region.

Irregular oblong shell with ribs radiating from beaks. Living shell covered with a short-haired brown periostracum. Exterior light brown with darker brown markings.

Strong shell with boat-shaped valves. Long straight hinge with numerous small teeth interrupted by the forward-facing beaks about a quarter of the way along from the front end. Beaks do not touch. Interior mother-of-pearl. Edible.

Attached to rocks and stones by strong threads (the byssus). Mediterranean and adjacent Atlantic in deeper water.

Cornered Ark Shell.

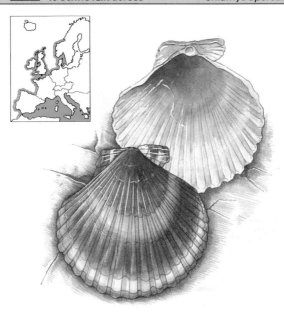

Almost circular shell with around 20 strong ribs. One of the 'ears' on either side of the beak is slightly longer than the other. Colour very variable, sometimes patterned.

Rounded arched shell with serrated edge. Hinge region has no teeth in mature shells. One central muscle scar on interior of valves. The animal swims by flapping the 2 valves open and shut.

Free-swimming, attached to rocks by strong threads (byssus) when very young, on the extreme lower shore to deeper water (around 200m:660ft). Common. Throughout the area (except Baltic).

Great Scallop; Variegated Scallop.

Off-white to brownish shell with a rounded beak, serrated edge and around 22 spiny ribs on each valve. Interior white, with flat ribs running some way in from edge.

Heavy arched shell, rounded-triangular in outline. Beak set well towards the anterior end. The living animal has a bright red foot, giving it an alternative common name of 'Red Nose'. Equal adductor muscle scars and no pallial sinus on interior.

Burrows just under the surface of sand, in shallow water and beyond. Empty shells generally found washed up on the beach. Throughout the area (except Baltic).

C. tuberculatum: very similar but ribs knobbed, not spiny; **Prickly Cockle:** to 5cm:2in long, fewer ribs spaced further apart, bearing small spines on anterior and near edge of shell only.

Rounded beaks coil forwards and away from the hinge, so that the whole shell is heart-shaped when viewed from the front.

Solid rounded arched shell with equal valves and a smooth edge. Off-white and covered with a dark brown periostracum. Interior white. Surface marked with fine concentric lines. No pallial sinus on interior. Edible.

Burrowing in sand or mud in shallow to deep water. Atlantic and Mediterranean.

None.

Spondylus gaederopus   to **10cm:4in** across

Cup-shaped lower valve attached to rocks has irregular spines and plate-like outgrowths. Flatter, ribbed, upper valve bears numerous long sharp spines. Red-brown to violet.

Large thick oval shell, a little broader than long, with small 'ears' at the hinge end. Interior shiny white, like porcelain. The hinge is of 2 interlocking teeth, and the 2 valves are difficult to prise apart.

On rocks in shallow to deeper water, Mediterranean and Portuguese coast.

None.

Irregular rounded greyish-brown shells, upper shell flat, resting inside saucer-shaped lower shell. Exterior of both ridged and fluted. Interior mother-of-pearl.

This well-known delicacy has declined considerably in numbers in some parts of the area. The shells are held together by an internal ligament and the hinge lacks teeth.

Lives attached to shelly or gravelly bottom in shallow water and down to 80m:260ft, in estuaries and inlets. Farmed commercially. Mediterranean, Atlantic, Channel, North Sea.

Portuguese Oyster: elongated, irregularly shaped; **Common Saddle Oyster.**

Blue-black ridged shell, pointed at one end, both parts similar, covered with a thin brown horny periostracum, and often encrusted with barnacles. Interior mother-of-pearl.

This edible mollusc with its bright orange gills attaches itself to the substrate by tough threads (the byssus). Tiny 'pearls' may occasionally be found inside. A filter-feeder, only mussels from unpolluted areas should be eaten.

Common on rocky shores and in estuaries, often forming extensive beds, from the middle shore down. Throughout the area.

Mediterranean Horse Mussel; Horse Mussel; Bearded Horse Mussel; Date Mussel.

Long narrow strongly curved shell, tapering towards the rear. Whitish, sometimes patterned red or brown. Surface covered with a shiny brownish-green periostracum.

Thin strong shell hinged near the front end and gaping at both ends. Anterior end rounded. Hinge has 1 tooth in one valve and 2 in the other. The live animal has a pale brown foot projecting from the anterior end of the shell.

On sandy beaches, burrowing in sand at low tide level and beyond, feeding through a short siphon projecting above the sand surface. Throughout the area (except Baltic).

E. arcuatus: grows up to 15cm:6in, only slightly curved, anterior end square-cut, live animal has a creamy-white foot; **Grooved Razor**; **Pod Razor**; *Pharus legumen*.

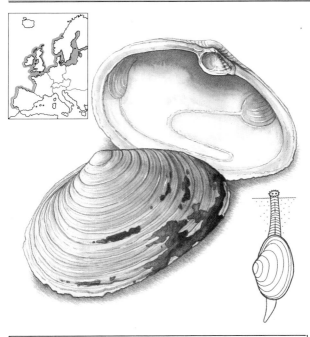

Large off-white chalky shell with a thin brown periostracum. Somewhat pointed rear end. Valves gape at both ends. Coarse concentric ridges on surface.

Oval thin shell with a rough surface. There is a spoon-shaped projection from the hinge region in the left valve only. Interior brownish. Pallial sinus present. The live animal has large long siphons enclosed in a horny sheath. Edible.

Burrows deeply in sand and mud. Common in estuaries, and from the intertidal zone to water 70m:230ft deep. Atlantic, Channel, North Sea and Baltic.

Blunt Gaper; Common Otter Shell and *Lutraria magna* (smaller): spoon-like projection in both valves.

Rather glossy smooth white to yellowish shell with concentric grooves. There is a spoon-shaped projection from the hinge region in both valves.

Large rather thin oblong-oval shell, valves gaping at both ends. Brownish-green horny periostracum. Interior white, pallial sinus present. A V-shaped tooth projects from hinge region of left valve.

Burrows in mud, sand or shell gravel. Found on the extreme lower shore and beyond to depths of 100m:330ft. Throughout the area (except Baltic).

Sand Gaper and **Blunt Gaper**: spoon-shaped projection in left valve only; other otter shells are also found in the area, e.g. *L. magna*: smaller (to 10cm:4in long).

Pecten maximus   to **15cm:6in** long

Reddish or yellowish circular shell, often mottled. Around 15 strong rounded ribs marked with fine longitudinal lines run from beak to the corrugated edge. 'Ears' are equal in size.

The largest scallop in European waters. The upper (left) valve is flat with a depression at the beak, the lower (right) valve is convex. Inside, wide flat ribs run in from edge. Hinge has no teeth. Edible, collected commercially.

Free-swimming, attached to a substrate by strong threads (byssus) only when young. A shell of deeper water, on a sandy or gravelly bottom. Atlantic, Channel and North Sea.

Pilgrim Scallop (*P. jacobaeus*) (**1**): very similar but slightly smaller (to 10cm:4in), ribs are more angular, Mediterranean; **Queen Scallop.**

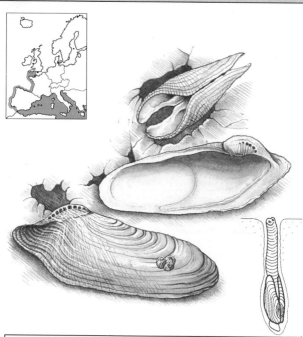

Grey-white elongated wing-like shell with numerous concentric and transverse ribs. The two halves are similar, with the beaks rolled back over onto the exterior. Interior white.

Rather light and fragile. The two valves gape widely at the front, and are joined only loosely by a ball joint on each. Chalky plates cover hinge region in living shell. The living animal is luminescent, giving off a blue-green light.

Bores deeply into rocks, wood or hard sand at low tide level and in shallow water, leaving a round hole from which its double siphon projects. A filter-feeder. Mediterranean, Atlantic north to southwestern Britain, Channel.

Oval Piddock and other smaller piddocks; **Flask Shell**. Other rock- and wood-boring shells include *Hiatella* spp., irregular oblong with a ridged surface, and the **Shipworm**.

HORSE MUSSEL

Modiolus modiolus to **15cm:6in** long (or smaller)

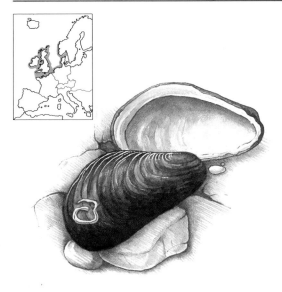

Purplish exterior, pearly white inside. Surface usually covered with a thick brown horny periostracum.

Thick elongated bluntly pointed shell with the beaks on the upper surface, not at the extreme anterior end. Unequal adductor muscle scars. Hinge region lacks teeth. The living animal is dark orange.

On rocks and amongst holdfasts of kelp, attached by tough threads (the byssus). On the extreme lower shore and beyond to depths of 150m:500ft. Atlantic north of the Bay of Biscay, Channel and North Sea.

Common Mussel; Mediterranean Mussel; Bearded Horse Mussel; Date Mussel.

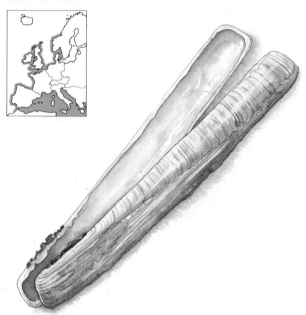

Long narrow rectangular whitish shell, with long edges straight and parallel to each other. Covered with a shiny greenish-yellow periostracum.

Thin strong shell hinged near the front end. Surface lined longitudinally and vertically. Periostracum often worn to a diagonal line across shell. Live animal has a creamy-white foot projecting from the anterior end.

On clean sandy beaches, burrowing in sand at low tide level and beyond, feeding through a siphon projecting above the sand surface. Throughout the area (except Baltic).

Sword Razor; Grooved Razor; *Pharus legumen*.

Pinna fragilis   to **30cm**:**12in** long

Heavy triangular brown shell, shaped like a fan. Surface concentrically lined and vertically ribbed.

One of the largest bivalves in European waters. No teeth in hinge. Interior glassy and iridescent. Stands upright, pointed end down, broad end projecting a little above surface of seabed.

In sand or gravelly mud, attached to a stone by strong threads (the byssus). Occasionally found on lower shore but usually in deeper water. Atlantic and North Sea.

A Mediterranean relative, the Rough Pen Shell (*P. nobilis*) is even larger (to 80cm:32in long), and is covered with overlapping scales.

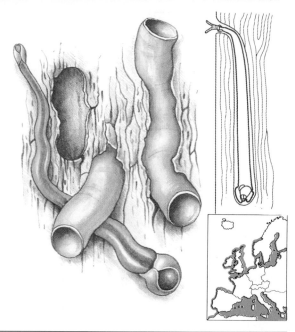

This worm-like mollusc has a much-reduced shell enclosing only a small part of the foot. The chalky white tubes are secreted by the animal as it bores through wood.

This wood-borer has been dreaded by sailors for centuries as it rapidly destroys ships' timbers and the wooden pilings of piers. The tiny fragile valves are rarely found. The siphon end is closed off by 2 small chalky plates or 'pallets'.

In submerged wood, boring by means of mechanical action of the valves. Throughout the region.

Several other species of shipworm are found in the region.

OTHER SMALL BIVALVES

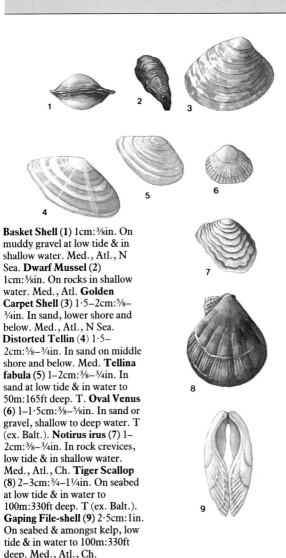

Basket Shell (1) 1cm:³⁄₈in. On muddy gravel at low tide & in shallow water. Med., Atl., N Sea. **Dwarf Mussel (2)** 1cm:³⁄₈in. On rocks in shallow water. Med., Atl. **Golden Carpet Shell (3)** 1·5–2cm:⁵⁄₈–³⁄₄in. In sand, lower shore and below. Med., Atl., N Sea. **Distorted Tellin (4)** 1·5–2cm:⁵⁄₈–³⁄₄in. In sand on middle shore and below. Med. **Tellina fabula (5)** 1–2cm:³⁄₈–³⁄₄in. In sand at low tide & in water to 50m:165ft deep. T. **Oval Venus (6)** 1–1·5cm:³⁄₈–⁵⁄₈in. In sand or gravel, shallow to deep water. T (ex. Balt.). **Notirus irus (7)** 1–2cm:³⁄₈–³⁄₄in. In rock crevices, low tide & in shallow water. Med., Atl., Ch. **Tiger Scallop (8)** 2–3cm:³⁄₄–1¹⁄₄in. On seabed at low tide & in water to 100m:330ft deep. T (ex. Balt.). **Gaping File-shell (9)** 2·5cm:1in. On seabed & amongst kelp, low tide & in water to 100m:330ft deep. Med., Atl., Ch.

Myrtea spinifera (1) 1–
2·5cm:⅜–1in. On muddy
seabed in shallow water. Med.,
Atl., Ch. **Faroe Sunset Shell** (2)
1–3·5cm:⅜–1⅜in. In sand,
lower shore & below. Med.,
Atl., N Sea. **Banded Venus** (3)
1–2·5cm:⅜–1in. In sand or
gravel on middle shore & below.
Round Double-tooth (4)
2·5cm:1in. On soft seabed,
offshore. Med., Atl., Ch. **Flask
Shell** (5) 2·5cm:1in. Boring into
rock or sand, low tide & in
shallow water. Med., Atl. **Paper
Thracia** (6) to 3cm:1¼in.
On sand at low tide & below. T (ex.
Balt.). **Baltic Tellin** (7)
2·5cm:1in. In muddy gravel,
tolerating low salinity. T.
Grooved Cardita (8) to
3cm:1¼in. Attached to stones &
rocks in shallow to deep water.
Med.

OTHER BIVALVES

Lagoon Cockle (1) 3–5cm:1¼–2in. In sand & mud in brackish water, tolerating low salinity. T. ***Gastrana fragilis*** (2) to 4·5cm:1¾in. In mud & sand in shallow water, in estuaries. Med., Atl. **Pandora Shell** (3) to 3·5cm:1⅜in. On surface of sand or mud on lower shore & in shallow water. Atl., Ch., N Sea. **Cornered Ark Shell** (4) to 5cm:2in. Attached to rocks on lower shore & in water to 100m:330ft deep. Med., Atl., Ch. **Smooth Scallop** (5) to 5cm:2in. Offshore, attached to rocks or free-living. Med. **Egg Cockle** (6) 3–6cm:1¼in–2½in. Offshore, in shell gravel. Med., Atl., N Sea. **Hairy Dog Cockle** (7) to 7cm:2¾in. In sand or mud in shallow to deep water. Med. **Banded Carpet Shell** (8) to 6cm:2½in. In sand & gravel at low tide & in shallow water. T (ex. Baltic).

OTHER BIVALVES

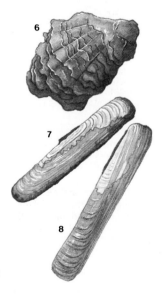

Mediterranean Mussel (1) to
10cm:4in. Forms beds on
middle shore & below. Med.,
Atl., Ch. **Bearded Horse
Mussel (2)** to 6cm:2⅜in. On
rocks & stones on lower shore &
below. T (ex. Balt.). **Oval
Piddock (3)** to 9cm:3½in.
Boring into soft rock & clay on
lower shore & in shallow water.
Atl., Ch., N Sea. **Blunt Gaper
(4)** to 7·5cm:3in. In mud & sand
on middle shore & beyond. Atl.,
Ch., N Sea. **Black Clam (5)**
9cm:3½in. In sand & mud at
low tide & beyond. T (ex.
Med.). **Portuguese Oyster (6)** to
15cm:6in. On rocks & gravel in
shallow water. Atl., Ch., N Sea.
Pharus legumen **(7)** to
12·5cm:5in. In sand at low tide
& in shallow water. Med., Atl.
Grooved Razor (8) to
12·5cm:5in. In sand, lower shore
& shallow water. T (ex. Balt.).

PAPER NAUTILUS

Argonauta argo   to **20cm:8in** long

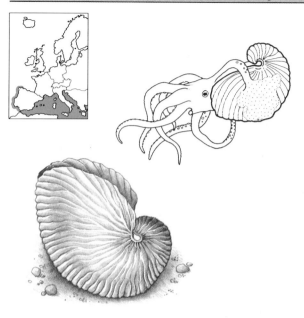

Thin translucent papery white cornucopia-shaped shell, ridged and furrowed and with a pronounced keel.

The 'shell' is produced by the female nautilus, a relative of the octopus and squid, and is only loosely attached to the body. Its main purpose is to hold the eggs.

Nautiloids crawl on the seabed or swim using their tentacles. An inhabitant of warm oceans worldwide, in Europe found in the Mediterranean and adjacent Atlantic.

None.

CHITONS

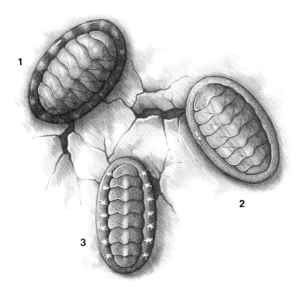

Chitons are flattened animals, elongated or rounded oval in shape. The shell consists of eight overlapping plates encircled by a fleshy girdle. Chitons live in the intertidal zone and in offshore waters, often in rock crevices or beneath rocks. They feed by scraping algae from the rocks. Most are less than 2cm:¾in long and are often overlooked. They are difficult to identify and those illustrated are a few of the commoner species.

Lepidochitona cinereus (**1**) One of the commonest chitons, found on most rocky shores between high and low tidemarks. Colour varies from grey to red to olive. Shell plates have a pronounced keel and are slightly granular.
Coat-of-Mail Chiton (*Lepidopleurus asellus*) (**2**) Smooth ash-grey plates with similarly coloured girdle. Lower shore and offshore. Atl., Ch., N Sea.
Acanthochitona crinitus (**3**) Rough brown to yellow plates with a central crest. Girdle edged with tufts of bristles. Lower shore and offshore. Atl., Ch., N Sea.

TUSK SHELL

Dentalium entalis   to **6cm:2⅜in** long

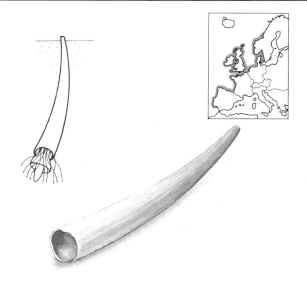

Tubular tapering curved shell like an elephant's tusk. White, sometimes tinged pink.

Smooth opaque solid shells, found washed up on the beach. Fine stripes fade out before the wider mouth. In the live animal a small 3-lobed foot and adhesive 'tentacles' project from the wider end.

A shell of deeper water, burrowing in sand or mud by means of its foot, with the narrow end of the shell projecting above the surface of the seabed. Atlantic, Channel and North Sea.

Similar related species live in the Mediterranean.

BARNACLES

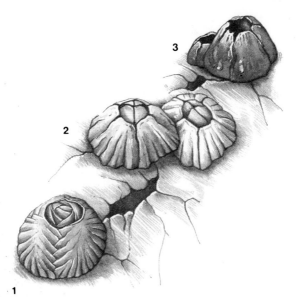

Unlike most of the other shells in this book, barnacles are not molluscs but crustaceans like crabs and shrimps. The shell is made up of several closely fitting chalky plates which close up tightly when exposed and open at the tip when under water, allowing the animal to put out the feathery appendages through which it feeds.

Verruca stroemia (**1**) to 0·5cm:³⁄₁₆in, often very flat, with 4 unequal diagonally ribbed outside plates. Colour grey, white or brown. Under stones and on shells, from lower shore down. Med., Ch., Atl., N Sea.

Acorn Barnacle (*Semibalanus balanoides*) (**2**) to 1·5cm:⅝in, flat or conical, 6 off-white plates surrounding a diamond-shaped opening. On rocks. Throughout, except Med. Other similar barnacles have differently shaped openings.

Balanus perforatus (**3**) to 3cm:1¼in across, a large, tall barnacle with 6 thick greyish-purple plates surrounding a jagged opening. On rocks, on the lower shore below Acorn Barnacle. Med. & Atl. north to Channel.

GOOSE BARNACLE

Lepas anatifera   to **5cm:2in** long

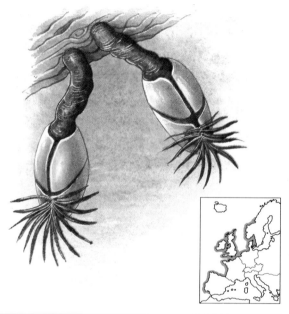

Shell made up of 5 translucent white plates with dark bluish reflections. Thick brownish-grey stalk up to 20cm:8in long can be partly drawn back into the shell.

Goose barnacles are crustaceans (like shrimps and crabs) not molluscs. The shell is made of close-fitting chalky plates which open at the tip when submerged, allowing the animal to put out its feathery feeding appendages.

Attached to submerged wood by means of the stalk, usually found on driftwood and the bottoms of boats. Atlantic, Channel and North Sea.

Other almost identical species are also commonly found. Also, *L. fascicularis:* smaller, washed up after gales on Atlantic coasts. Several individuals are attached by their stalks to a spongy float secreted by the animals.

Index and Checklist

All species in Roman type are illustrated.
Keep a record of your findings by ticking the boxes.